THE
PLATE
THAT BROKE
THE WORLD
ONE MAN'S JOURNEY INTO THE EGO

TUCKER BEARDEN

Copyright © 2021 By Tucker Bearden

THE PLATE THAT BROKE THE WORLD

All rights reserved. No part of this publication may be reproduced, distributed, or transmitted in any form or by any means, including photocopying, recording, or other electronic or mechanical methods, without the prior written permission of the publisher, except in the case of brief quotations embodied in critical reviews and certain other noncommercial uses permitted by copyright law. For permission requests, write to the publisher, addressed "Attention: Permissions Coordinator," at info@beyondpublishing.net

"All quotes are from A Course in Miracles, copyright ©1992, 1999, 2007 by the Foundation for Inner Peace, 448 Ignacio Blvd #306 Novato, CA 94949, www.acim.org and info@acim.org, used with permission."

Quantity sales special discounts are available on quantity purchases by corporations, associations, and others. For details, contact the publisher at the address above.

Orders by U.S. trade bookstores and wholesalers. Email info@BeyondPublishing.net

The Beyond Publishing Speakers Bureau can bring authors to your live event. For more information or to book an event contact the Beyond Publishing Speakers Bureau speak@BeyondPublishing.net

The Author can be reached directly at BeyondPublishing.net

Manufactured and printed in the United States of America distributed globally by BeyondPublishing.net

New York | Los Angeles | London | Sydney

ISBN Hardcover: 978-1-637920-52-7

ISBN Softcover: 978-1-637920-27-5

TABLE OF CONTENTS

Foreword	*Where Did This Book Get its Name?*	7
Chapter One	*The Smallest Pebbles: The Biggest Waves*	9
Chapter Two	*The Void: A Safe Place*	15
Chapter Three	*The Plate Concept: Visualization Of a Process*	21
Chapter Four	*False Tethers*	25
Chapter Five	*Locating The Loop*	29
Chapter Six	*The Ego Barrier*	33
Chapter Seven	*The Ten-Year Rule*	37
Chapter Eight	*No Losses, Only Lessons*	39

FOREWORD

WHERE DID THIS BOOK GET ITS NAME?

I wish I could take credit for the naming of this book but, unfortunately, I cannot. While looking for a second opinion as to how I was doing on it, I sent my manuscript to a close friend by the name of Joshua Colella. I explained to him how I had drawn out the idea on a paper plate to show my girlfriend at the time.

He read the manuscript and had this to say "When my best friend Tucker reached out to me to tell me he was writing a new book, I was excited. He told me he had discovered the secret to relationships in his void. I became intrigued because at that time I was going through my own challenges in my marriage of 15 years. I was the first person to read it as Tucker finished each chapter. With each chapter it started to become clearer and clearer to me that what I was reading was life changing. I started understanding the plate and how it effects us on many different levels, both personally and professionally. It was then, I realized I had a new understanding that I could use to start rebuilding a destroyed relationship with my own mother, that I had abandoned and condemned long ago. After finishing the book, it hit me that it's the lack of knowledge and understanding, of the plate that's found in the pages of this book, that was destroying all relationships in our lives. That's how the title "The Plate That Broke The World" came to me. Because of wisdom found in this book, I have taken major steps to rebuild what seemed to be a lost and hopeless relationship with my mother. This book can be life changing if you apply the lessons. Thank you Tucker." So The Plate That Broke The World was born!

CHAPTER ONE

THE SMALLEST PEBBLES: THE BIGGEST WAVES

No one asked to be brought into this world. It wasn't a multiple-choice question with options to choose from. You didn't get to choose your family, your gender, or your skin tone. These things were given to you by a power greater than we may ever know. Being that we had no say in our creation, we have no right to ask with any state of expectancy for things to be easy. But we do have the right to become whatever is required of us to make it easier. Along the way, you will find that no matter how cautious you may be, no matter who you become, stones will find their way onto your plate. Where they fall from, who knows. These things represent offsets in life. The challenges we face, big or small. It often feels as if the weight of it all is going to break the plate altogether, but I am here to tell you that there is a better way.

In life, we have many beginnings and oftentimes, just as many endings. If we get lucky along the way, the ladder will fall short of the former for some time and leave us with a series of lasting changes that might include relationships, titles, beliefs, and the other things. Everything that has a beginning must have an end, but there are two types of endings in this world. There are those taken by time and those taken by actions. A relationship broken by the passing of a lover is one taken by time; whereas, a relationship broken by dishonesty or unfaithfulness is one taken by actions.

In the beginning, boulders barely make waves. But upon the passing of time, even pebbles are capable of stirring up tsunamis. A chaotic reality for many, but not set in stone for the few. The few who know the truth that lies before you today. The few who understand the principles you now hold in your possession. Coming to understand what you have here will allow you to choose what kind of ending your story will have. This... this is part of my story.

My name is Tucker Bearden, and I have a neurological abnormality known as Asperger's syndrome. It hinders my natural ability to understand social cues, emotional responses, and things like sarcasm. I know that some people believe in removing that title, but I am proud to be an Aspie, so that will never change. Throughout a series of events in my life, I have become a public speaker and authority in the field of Asperger's syndrome, its challenges, gifts, struggles, and blessings. I have shared stages with Les Brown, Brian Tracy, Sharon Lechter, and many other greats. I am blessed and truly love what I do.

When I speak at an event, I don't just show up and speak from stage. I always find the host and ask them two simple questions. First, "Mr./Mrs. Host, would you mind speaking with me after the event, so I may give my feedback and video testimonial?" They will almost always say yes. Next, I ask them "Mr./Mrs. Host, I see everyone getting ready to set up the event. Would you mind if I pitched in and help put things together?" They will ALWAYS say yes to this one. Remember, be the blessing for others, and you will live within blessings.

While helping set up one of these events, I met a young lady who would, for a short time, become part of my journey and will not soon be forgotten. We were not made for one another, but you learn something from every person you come across in this world, and you should treasure every part of the process, no matter how hard that is sometimes. Our passion was short-lived, but the lessons learned will last forever.

She lit up the room when she walked in, putting a smile on everyone's face, making them feel warm and welcome. Over and over again, I would find myself noticing her over everyone else in the room, and there were over four hundred guests that day. Never had I felt such a magnetism with anyone before. It scared me and caught me off guard, so I kept my distance the best I could. I hadn't come to the event to find a mate, I had come to inspire and teach.

Well, apparently, she felt the same way as I did. We tried to divert from one another, but the more we pushed, the stronger the pull became. So, I took a leap of faith while riding in an elevator and asked, "May I kiss you?" She said "yes," and the journey of writing this book began. As all relationships do, we blossomed in the beginning. It seemed like there was no wrong either of us could do, and every day was an adventure full of wonder and bliss. I couldn't wait to see a text message or call from her. She couldn't stand the thought of being away from me.

It was a spark. That spark we feel when we get the idea to start a new business, when we meet someone new, or when we accomplish something meaningful. It brings light to a darkness we couldn't bare in some way. That's why it's special. It's almost a feeling of lucidity or clarity that wasn't there before. I had been in a very dark place for a long time before the Universe blessed me with my little spark. Oftentimes, our greatest blessings will come to us within our darkest hours. And within these blessings, you will find strength beyond measure.

In the beginning, we didn't argue or fight. No matter what came at us, we brushed it off, and the spark burned bright. Boulders barely made waves. Anyone who has ever been in a relationship of any degree has experienced this. That feeling of invincibility you get when it's new. It is exciting and engulfs your mind. It becomes the only thing you can think about. But the new wears off at some point. What's left then is the person you will come to know and possibly love.

Before long, the insignificant faults that weren't noticeable before began getting under our skin and causing us to fight. We would bicker and argue over the smallest things. Things that meant nothing would blow up into huge arguments that would leave both of us feeling broken. Upon the passing of time, even pebbles are capable of stirring up tsunamis. The old wise ones say that it eventually happens to everyone. The trick is finding your way back to the spark. But I know, I know, it's easier said than done.

So, I began taking note of any and everything I could to do a full-on psychoanalyze of both of us to figure out why this was occurring. I went to friends looking for advice, and they all said the same thing, "This is just part of it. Welcome to relationships." Then, they would laugh, and I would again walk away, no closer to figuring it out than I was before.

I searched to find what was triggering our fights on both sides. There had to be an answer. Just because other people had accepted the reality they created for themselves, doesn't mean that we have to as well. I went looking for answers. People would laugh and say, "Happy wife, happy life," then leave it be. It seems like people laugh a lot after saying something that makes them feel slightly uncomfortable. Possibly because they know that it pokes at a question they have no answer to. People don't like not knowing the answer, so they accept what they can. Laughter often moves the conversation on without much effort. It reminds me of the old saying, "When a wise man speaks amongst fools, he shall hear nothing but laughter. Yet when a fool speaks amongst the wise, he shall hear nothing."

After a while, I came to find that when we fought, I would try to explain how she made me feel in the moment, and it made her think I was judging her in some way. She would say things when angry that made me feel less than a man. We held onto those things and created connections to false belief systems that we thought we had for one another. In the process of doing so, without knowing it, we were threatening each other's egos. You will come to find that very few people who become emotionally invested in that department walk away unscathed. When tampering with one's ego, you are poking a tiger with a stick. So, the real source of our bickering was not the often meaningless things that stimulated arguments. The source of our problems was a compilation of scars carved onto the walls of our ego.

Now, figuring this part out is all fine and dandy, but what do you do with it? You have to find a way to relay your message without your partner's defenses going up. We all know that once the hornet's nest is shook up, it isn't easy to move it. I had to find a way to not only explain this to her, but to myself. I couldn't shake the feeling that I had stumbled upon something. But what was it? I had a lot of questions, so I took them to the one place I knew would have the answers. And no, it was not Google.

CHAPTER TWO

THE VOID: A SAFE PLACE

There is a place I go in my mind that I refer to as "the void". It is a vast white space where sound echoes and theories are tested. But no one knows what happens there. Other than the painter holding the brush, no one dares roam there. And for good reason. Just as a blank canvass is a home to a painter's brush, the void is my place of creation. Free from prying eyes, saturated misunderstandings, and judgment. I am free to do and create as I please here. It is mine alone.

Within the void, I can build machines, inventions, and concepts, then test them to see if they will work before building them in real life. If it works in the void, it works in the world. When things get out of control, I simply wipe the slate clean and start over. But sometimes, it isn't easy to erase everything. Sometimes, I lose control. See, when you create things within the void, they tend to take on a life of their own. Almost like a program. You bring the pieces and push play. What happens from there on is up to chance. There are creatures I have created here that ended up stuck in my subconscious mind, as if they were a virus I stumbled upon and couldn't shake off.

I have learned to be cautious as to what I allow to fester here. That is the beauty of it though. Life... the void breathes life into ideas prior to conception. If they didn't do as they please, it wouldn't be real, would it? If they didn't take on a life of their own—whether mechanical or otherwise—it wouldn't be an experiment, would it? It would be like sitting at the controls of a video game making the avatar move as you please. That pre-programmed response defeats the purpose. It's funny when you think about it: isn't that what God or whatever higher power you believe in did? Thought us into existence to see what would happen. Gave us free will, sat back with a bucket of popcorn and a lawn chair, then pushed play. Just another bit of code in the program. But I digress.

Below, you will come to realize that within the void, though it is in your mind and a part of you, you are within it, and in turn, you follow its flow. The concept is simple. You bring what information you have and release it to the void with a set intention or goal in mind, then let the laws of cause and effect do as they please. To go there, I simply close my eyes and open my mind. Once in the void, I released all the information I had obtained about my partner and me. I set my intention to find an answer. Not knowing what would happen or how it would turn out, I let go. While standing in the blank space, colors, clouds, and blurred memories swirled around me from every direction. For a short while, I watched as the different clips, images and sounds scrolled through one another like an old film wheel.

Then, everything stopped, and I could see two large, rotating circles revolving around a singular point of focus. One circle had a slightly smaller radius than the other. The smaller one was inside the larger of the two. The space that made up the inside of this circle was empty second to a dot at the very center. Then outside of the circle, I noticed trees that seemed to be placed at random with no known connection to one another. They surrounded the rotating circle with seemingly no rhyme, pattern, or reason.

To get a better view, I walked under this rotating circle. While looking up at the center point, I realized that the circle wasn't a circle at all, but a two-dimensional rotating disk. Curiously enough, I didn't notice this before, due to my perspective. Not yet grasping what I was looking at, something strange happened. I began to notice small rocks falling from above and landing on this disk as it rotated.

Some of them were large, and some of them were small, but all of them would inevitably get flung off of the edge of the disk as it continued to spin. As each stone made its way flying off the sides, it would often collide with one or two of the trees before hitting the ground and vanishing. They didn't seem to do much damage, but some of the trees would fall and others would move. Some would just stand still.

While looking across the field below this rotating disk, I saw that young lady standing alone with her head down and arms crossed, sobbing. She also had a disk above her, but it was moving slowly and looked clustered. I could see the tears falling, but no matter how much I tried to move closer, she was always on the other side. Always out of my reach. I shouted, and though it echoed through the void like a vast cavern, she did not hear my cries.

Confused and a bit disoriented, I looked back up. Something had changed. Something was wrong. The rocks were still falling, but as they landed, tethers were being attached to them that were connected to the center point. Like ropes that hold a boat to its dock, the tethers tangled the rocks, allowing no stone to escape. The disk still rotated, but was now weighed down and moving much slower than before.

A few moments passed. Then, the rocks began making their way off the sides, creating a carousel effect. More and more rocks fell over the edge. Each with a rope tied tightly around it. As the disk rotated, the rocks gained momentum, eventually sticking out past the rim, as if they were hanging onto the ropes for dear life. Each rope slowly got longer and longer until one after another, they began tangling up in the trees surrounding the disk.

Before I knew it, the tangled mess had halted the rotation of the disk altogether. Now, even if I could have gotten closer to her, there were so many tethers that I wouldn't be able to navigate through them. There were so many that they blocked out the light, leaving a shadow in their wake, creating a darkness I could feel in my gut. She was gone, and there was nothing I could do to change that.

Suddenly, the space between the large outer rim and the smaller inner circle began to light up like heated metal. It glowed and rotated free from the tangled tethers as it burned them in half, releasing the stones all at once. The glowing ring rotated violently in one direction as the disk pulsated and rotated in the opposite direction faster than it ever had before. Now, the rocks that fall onto the disk are being shattered on contact. And for the ones that do make it to the edge, that heated ring severs any ties that may have been created along the way. Nothing but the dot remains. Nothing but the center of focus that the disk rotates around.

At that moment, I looked back across the field to see her standing only a few feet away smiling with arms out wide. We hugged the same way we did in the beginning. We held each other in an embrace. It was as if I left for the war and had just come home for the first time. I didn't want to let her go, ever again. I never wanted to feel helpless again. I never wanted to see her cry or be out of reach again.

While holding her in my arms and thinking about what this all could mean, it came to me in a flash! I understood it all! I held her face, kissed her, and exclaimed, "I GOT IT!" Then, I came back to reality with a fire lit in my soul. It was one of those "aha" moments that you can feel in your spirit. Everything was about to change.

CHAPTER THREE

THE PLATE CONCEPT: VISUALIZATION OF A PROCESS

Once I had a thorough understanding of the concept, I had to find a way to put it into a layman perspective that anyone could understand. It has been said that genius defines an action, not a person. Genius is not the act of taking something simple and complicating it. It is the act of taking something complicated and simplifying it. Everyone is capable of genius acts and has them. The question is whether or not a person sees them or lets them slip.

So, what had happened in the void that day, and what—if anything—did all of it mean? It isn't very often that I sit down and try to write out what happens there, but I will do my best, so stay with me. In the shortest sense I can imagine, what happened was that I created a three-dimensional visualization of a process of operations within the subconscious mind to more accurately assess and understand its inner workings. When I was in school, I did this with math. I haven't the slightest clue how to solve a mathematical equation on paper, but within the void, I can solve almost anything thrown at me. Just don't ask me to write it out for you, because I won't be able to show you how I got the answer. Thankfully, this isn't math, and I found a way to explain it on paper, so here is the breakdown.

First, we will start with the dot or point of focus. The dot represents us, the self, or the atman. You as you are within your plane of existence. It is very important to remember that no matter what, you must come back to the dot when things get off balance. You must come back to yourself. We often exert exhausting amounts of energy on simplifying the lives of others while complicating our own in the process. This is not a fault in your code, but a gift that's energy has yet to be properly focused. I will never tell you not to help people, because there is no greater purpose than service to others. What I will suggest is that you bless people along your path to self-development and independence, but do not alter your path tending to someone else's garden only to see your roses whither.

The second part of visualizing this process is seeing the space between the dot and the edge of the plate. That seemingly empty place. It is the here, the now, this moment. The space that makes up everything around the dot is at it is, not by chance, but by design. Anything that has happened is happening or ever did happen outside of this very moment is irrelevant. That space on the plate is always empty until you decide to drop a heaping helping of nonsense on it. Always keep in mind that your garden will grow what you plant within this place. If you plant seeds from the past, you will fight weeds of depression that block out the sun. If, on the other hand, you focus on seeds that have yet to be sowed, you will bear the thorns of anxiety. See, it's okay to look over the edge every now and then, but only to look. Stay within the now.

I once read a story somewhere of two monks walking along when they spotted a young woman with a long kimono trying to cross a road. The road had a puddle of mud in it, so the older monk picked her up, carried her across the road, sat her down, and continued on his way. Four hours passed as they were walking in silence, meditating. Then, suddenly, with a tone of obvious disapproval, the younger monk spoke up, "You picked up that woman back there. We are not supposed to touch women. It is against our vows." The older monk stopped, "I sat that woman down four hours ago and yet you are still carrying her. Let it go."

This story helps remind us to come back to the moment. When stones fall onto your plate—and they will—you must be able to deflect them. The plate is in constant motion. It rotates around its center, no matter where it goes. That motion is the life force that keeps everything in balance. Rocks of all shapes and sizes will fall onto your plate, but if it is spinning fast enough, they will simply slide off of the sides and into the abyss. On the other hand, if your plate has slowed down, you will find it difficult to move the stones. They will pile up until all you see is rubble. The plate will slowly stop turning until the darkest corners of your mind open up, breathing life to depression, anxiety, and anger, without any repression in sight.

Never allow memories of past pains to rob you of your present joy. Ten years from now, that thing that happened, that thing they said, that you said, that you did, won't even be on your mind. If it will not be important then, do not give it power over you today. You cannot change the past, but you can accept that it will not change and move on. People are going to say and do things in your life that cut deep. It is okay to take time to heal that wound, but the plate has to keep moving and that stone has to be removed. Some stones are so large that it seems impossible to move them, but if you stay in motion, the stone has no choice but to work its way off of your plate. Some take longer than others, and that is okay, but time is of the essence, so make haste.

CHAPTER FOUR

FALSE TETHERS

Now, to keep the plate moving, we must first understand what makes it move faster just as well as what makes it slow down. I believe a wonderful representation of the concept we are currently addressing would go as follows. The horse trots where you lead it, but now and then, without asking, it takes shelter under a tree before it rains. This moment will always be this moment, no matter how much it seems that it is moving with us. It is as it is, where it is when it was, and as it always will be. You do not control it, just as you do not control a horse. Horses are large, powerful animals. You can make suggestions for them to move, creating some false sense of control in the process. But even the clown knows it's all a joke.

Many things will happen outside of our control. People don't like not being in control. It makes them uneasy. Honestly, to always be in control would defeat the whole purpose, don't you think? It would all be rather boring if you ask me. So, in some odd sense, you must learn to appreciate the things that break your illusion of control. See them as they are and find value in the alterations they create along the way. What crumbles your castle today may very well be preparing the land for a palace to be built tomorrow. It always strikes a nerve with the rider at first when a horse stops following his lead to walk under a tree. But as the rain comes down only moments later, you will see the rider smile, pet his horse, and say "good job." The moment does not follow your guidance because it just is. But it has never vocally opposed the suggestion. Let the horse graze, but never forget to bring her home when the rain is gone.

When things happen in our lives, we often create false tethers, unrealistic ties connecting the actions of our lower self to the atman or higher self. Imagine if you will, the stones falling off the plate, but now, instead of them falling into the abyss, they are connected to the center of the plate by ropes that will not let them go. As your plate rotates, these stones will gain momentum and stretch out beyond its horizons. Visually speaking, this would create a carousel effect with rocks stretched out in every direction.

The more of these rocks that you accumulate, the more energy is required to keep the plate in motion. This puts a strain on the system. This slows it down. The false tethers you create in your mind bind you to a reality outside of your desired sense of control. We must also keep in mind that beyond the outer edges of the plate are trees growing all about in every direction. These trees represent all of the different projects you are working on, connections you are building, people you are growing with, opportunities, all instances outside of this current moment. Trees have the ability to grow large and strong, just as they have the ability to die and be forgotten, so always be mindful of what trees you tend to in your garden. Apple trees will never disappoint, because you know the fruit it bears. Weeds often have some of the most beautiful flowers, but they will drain your garden of everything and leave it barren.

When you maintain false tethers, the stones pick up a lot of momentum, swinging around the plate. Eventually, you will find that they not only collide with everything around you, but tangle up in the branches of and destroy many of the seeds you worked so hard to plant in your garden. They wrap around a tree here and break a branch there. Little by little, one by one, they alter everything in their wake. Once enough of these tethers are tangled up, your garden will closely resemble the web of an oddly confused spider or a dream catcher that lacks any specific design. If you have ever seen a string wrapped up in the spokes of a bicycle tire, you will have witnessed this. How quickly the plate can come to a grinding halt.

Once the plate stops turning, everything falls apart. This is where breakups, emotional outbursts, and mental breakdowns happen. It probably wouldn't be far from the truth to say that you have experienced this at one point or another. Someone does something that gets under your skin, and you let it go in the moment, but every day, the thought festers in your mind. The agitation builds up until you can't take it, and for the most insignificant reason, you snap! You tell them all the horrible things you have been thinking and really let 'em have it. This is a perfect example of too many tethers and too many stones on someone's plate.

But that's really it, isn't it...the "it" of it all, so to speak. See, each strand may not seem like much, but enough strands make up a rope. It only takes one of those ropes to tangle everything up. If you don't let those stones go, the combination of all your problems, dramas, pains, and past experiences will run amuck. Out of control. And as they whirl about, ripping up your garden, it is wise to keep in mind that the wave of your stones passing will forever alter the very essence of the people it leaves within its wake. The small pebbles you throw into life's pond may not seem like much today, but in some world and in some way, things will never be the same, because you came this way.

CHAPTER FIVE

LOCATING THE LOOP

Believe it or not, there is a science behind why we create such tethers and hold onto negative memories for so long. It is a survival mechanism known as "negativity bias". The trait evolved to keep us alive by assuming the worst and making it easier for your brain to recall negative experiences than positive ones. It's easy to understand why these traits exist. Let's say you were walking down the road at night and a hooded figure started bee lining towards you. Most people would assume the person was a threat and change their course. If the person ended up just being a jogger, you might look silly, but if they were a threat and you had stayed, that could be the last mistake you ever made. Thousands of years ago, it may have been a tiger. Simply put, through successive generations of natural selection, those who assumed an inherently cautious view of the world were more likely to survive. This is why the negativity bias trait still plagues our brains today.

Modern science has confirmed the existence of negativity bias. In one neurological study, participants were shown a series of positive, negative, or neutral images. The negative images triggered higher levels of electrical activity in the brain. This may not sound like a big deal, but this directly impacts the way we see the world, and consequently, how we behave. Negative events are much more salient. Hence, why some people end up in therapy because they think their entire life is a train wreck when, in fact, most of life consists of positive experiences. Only, they're long forgotten at the expense of the negative ones.

Do you ever find yourself ruminating over past events or worrying about what's going to happen in the future? Of course, you do. Not because you're sick in the head or need medication. Your past haunts you because you're human and your brain is pre-programmed to find the negative in life. The thing is that this survival mechanism isn't as useful as it used to be. Unless you live in the jungle, you're unlikely to spend your days worrying about tigers. Instead, you'll be obsessing over the possibility of losing your relationships, your job, or your money.

Worry might seem sensible in the moment. It may even motivate you to work harder. But it's not going to bring you happiness or peace of mind. It actually releases a chemical in the brain known as cortisol. It is the primary stress hormone. Cortisol increases sugars (glucose) in the bloodstream, enhances your brain's use of glucose, and increases the availability of substances that repair tissues. Unfortunately, it also curbs functions that would be nonessential or detrimental in a fight-or-flight situation. This includes your immune system and your ability to make good decisions. Hence, why you get headaches and say things or do things you may not normally do when stressed out.

When you are blissfully happy or in a flow states, your brain is filled with a cocktail of neurochemicals that make you feel alert and ecstatic. Norepinephrine heightens your concentration. Dopamine improves your cognitive alertness. Endorphins activate the opioid receptor, which, along with anandamide brings on the feeling of bliss. Serotonin lifts your mood. Finally, a good shot of oxytocin, the love hormone, leaves you with a sort of post-orgasmic glow. Smiling, laughing, and enjoying the time you have with those you hold in high regard will not only improve your professional and personal relationships, but your health as well.

The human brain is the most complex organism in the known universe. It creates connections and networks we may never fully understand. Due to negativity bias, it creates something known as a loop in the subconscious mind. Like the symbol that represents infinity, it always comes back around to the same place. When a loop is allowed to complete itself, it throws your plate off balance and leads to depression, anxiety, anger, and destruction. So, what is it? What is a loop? A loop is a mental treadmill you hop on that wears you out, but doesn't take you anywhere. It is the process that weaves the tethers, themselves, together, strengthening their bonds to the stones we so desperately need to let go of. It is that nightmare you keep replaying, even though it always ends up leaving you in a bad mood and messes up your day. It is that story you told yourself right before you acted out of line and made a horrible decision. It's that anger and pain-driven memory that just won't seem to stop.

When you find yourself thinking about a negative experience you had in the past or are anticipating one you may have in the future, you are beginning the process of creating a loop. Whether you were aware of it or not, this is something everyone has done at some point. Think back to a time when you were pacing back and forth in your room, thinking about some bad experience you had. Someone did or said something to you. You did or said something to someone else. You start to play the memory back over in your head, as if it were a movie you were obligated to finish. Saying in your mind what you "should" have said, doing what you "should" have or could have done. Changing little details until you are the victor within your fantasy. We have all done it.

It may seem like a harmless thought experiment, but the effects from it can last a lifetime. Doing it once and letting it go is natural. What makes it a loop is playing it over and over again, as if there were some potential for a different result. Insanity at its finest. Like a song stuck in your head, it plays and plays until finally, you give in. You go look up that song to listen to it, or you act on whatever has been festering in the back of your mind. For a relationship, it may be an argument or a breakup. For a job, it may be quitting without notice. For a business, it may be firing someone who probably would have made a great part of the team if you had calmed your head and only given them a chance.

In order to keep loops from being completed, it takes a bit of practice and time. I like to remember three key phrases: shoulda, coulda, and woulda. If you catch yourself saying any of these three things in your head while going over a negative memory in your mind, stop yourself. You will feel a sudden urge and obligation to finish the thought first, but it is important to stop yourself cold. Those three phrases are always there when loops are created. I should have said this. I could have done that. I would have done this if... Let it go.

Going back and forth in your head, playing those bad memories, is like drinking poison and hoping it kills a long-lost enemy or changes the past in some way. That enemy that will never know your suffering, nor be touched by your anger. The past is as it was and as it always will be. We cannot change the past, but we can accept that it will not change and move on. If not, that poison will taint the very soil of your garden. Blackening the roots of your trees and slowly draining the life from every last seed you sow. So, take a deep breath in, and just let it go. Break the loop and come back to this moment, because that's really all there is.

CHAPTER SIX

THE EGO BARRIER

In order to protect your garden, it is paramount that you break the loops and cut ties with each stone before it has a chance to wreak havoc. Stones that weigh down your plate cannot be left to chance. They throw things off balance. Nothing new will ever be allowed to grow so long as your garden is constantly being bombarded by stones of the past and tangled up by tethers of a distant reality. So, we create something one might call an ego barrier around the plate. I like to imagine a red-hot ring oscillating just beyond this present moment. Stones will still fall as they always do, but any connections to them will be cut by the barrier at the edge of your plate. Everything comes back to the dot in the center. Everything comes back to balance. Once this happens, you will experience a euphoric sense of release known as nirvana.

Take a moment to imagine the ropes tying you to your heaviest burdens being burned away. Nothing outside of now is real. When you find yourself drifting off balance, you will always find accompanied by that feeling, a tether yet to be broken. It is unrealistic to think that life can or ever will be perfect all of the time. There will be times when you do things you regret or argue with someone and they say something that rips into your ego, leaving that ever-so-lovely turning feeling in your gut. Do not create false connections to these things and let them weigh you down outside of now. It is okay to respond emotionally to something, but once it has passed, let it go and come back to the present.

For example, if you and someone get into an argument, one of you—if not both of you—will say things while angry that makes the other feel less than. When hurtful things are said or done, we mustn't create lasting connections from what was said to who we are or our beliefs about ourselves. Let it rotate off of the plate and once it is gone, let it go. Your ego barrier cuts any ties you may have had. Say you make a fool of yourself or fail at something important. A wise man once said, "Shit happens." Once it has happened, you cannot change it, so do not give it the pleasure of changing you into something you never wanted to be. Let it go, and stay in motion.

The process of creating your ego barrier starts with setting a standard for yourself. No great change in our life ever really occurs without some form of standard or paradigm shift. When someone decides to quit smoking and really decides to stop, they set a standard for themselves that says, "No more!" They draw a line in the sand and say, "No matter what, I will not cross that line again." I set a standard for myself to write this book. No matter what, I work on this book every day in some way. Once you set a standard for yourself, backed up by a sold why, you would be shocked at what you can accomplish in this world.

Now, it is all fine and dandy to set a better standard for yourself, but if it isn't backed up by a "why" that truly matters, you will fall short every time. I quit smoking cigarettes after smoking two-and-a-half packs a day for six years. But it wasn't until I had a good enough reason that it stuck. One night while walking back to the barn I was living in at the time, it was snowing, and I could barely breathe. I can remember running through the snow when I was a young boy just fine, yet I couldn't even walk in the cold without losing my breath. I was disgusted by where I had allowed my health to get. If I didn't do something, I would never be able to do many of the things I have on my bucket list, like running in a cross-country race or climbing the misty mountains of Japan. So, I set a standard for myself and said that I would never stoop lower than it again. I love myself too much to lower my standards.

There has to be a reason for your ego barrier as well. My reason for wanting to stay in the moment is simple. I have experienced the darkness, anxiety, and pain that comes with living outside of now, and I have no reason to go back. Before discovering this concept, I would have life-threatening panic attacks by simply going to the grocery store. I was living in a world where I created false connections to every stone that fell on my plate, and in turn, I laid waste to everything along my path. Pain is a teacher whose lessons are more rarely forgotten.

For you, the reason could be any number of things. You may be suffering from depression due to the stones you have accumulated over the years. You may be having trouble with your spouse and have created false connections about them or vice versa. No matter where you are in life, no matter what tethers have been tangling up your garden, you can release those burdens and be free to move at your own pace. You have to decide that once something has happened, it is gone and it as if it never was. Let it go. When you begin doing this, your garden will grow like never before. No longer will petty arguments or failures hold you back from your true potential. No longer will your past weigh down your present.

CHAPTER SEVEN

THE TEN-YEAR RULE

In our lives, we are going to experience a vast array of shortcomings, victories, and lessons. Over time, you may notice that most of those experiences are forgotten and left to fade away. The ones that stick always have a purpose. There are two kinds of experiences in this world. There are high-level experiences, and there are low-level experiences. A low-level experience would be riding a roller coaster. It is fun, and we may take pictures to hang on our walls, but the memory will be forgotten years down the road.

Another example of a low-level experience would be arguing with your spouse, co-worker, or business partner. Any time this kind of thing happens, stop yourself and think about how quickly the problem could be solved by stepping behind your ego barrier and letting it go. Make the right choice by letting go, and this moment won't even be remembered ten years from now. Make the wrong choice by holding on, and this one moment could very well alter the rest of your life.

A high-level experience is one that leaves a lasting impact for years to come. For example, let's say that you and your friends were to climb Mount Everest and went through hell to make it there and back. Would you forget that very easily? No. It would end up being the topic of conversation everywhere you go. It would be something that would remain in your mind ten, twenty, or even fifty years from that moment. This happens when something changes who you are and how you see the world in some way. We call this a paradigm shift, and paradigm shifts make us who we are.

It isn't always easy to let go of the things on our plate, so I developed a method to help remove unwanted stones and nonsense. I call it the ten-year rule. The ten-year rule is very simple, yet profound. If it will not be bothering you ten years from now, do not give it power over you in this moment. Sometimes, I like to close my eyes and imagine a version of myself ten years from now standing before me. I ask him if he would be proud of me for what I am about to do, and if the answer is "no," I do not do it. The meal you ate on your plate at thanksgiving three years ago isn't there anymore. You threw away the garbage and washed your plate. The plate doesn't hold a grudge or remember how bad aunt Sue's pie was. Just as the plate does not judge what we put on it, we cannot judge ourselves for what has come to pass. We are not perfect, and that is okay. Because sometimes, it's okay to just not be okay.

CHAPTER EIGHT

NO LOSSES, ONLY LESSONS

I grew up on an old dirt road, and it taught me many lessons. One of which is that the only clear path is forward. If you have ever had the pleasure of driving down a dirt road, you may have noticed that looking in your rearview mirror does you no justice. The dust is so thick that it clouds everything behind you, so there is no way of seeing where you were only moments ago. If you abruptly stop, the dust will consume you until there is no clear way out. But once you begin moving forward again, the dust fades away, and the path becomes clear. The only way is forward.

The young lady I met all that time ago was not meant to be the one for me, but I would not trade the time we spent together for the world. A great friend of mine named Jake Love taught me something that stuck in my mind and has served me well in some of my darkest hours; "In life, there are no losses, only lessons". We had different dreams and though things didn't work out between us, the experience leads us to where we are today. Without her contribution, this book would have never been written, and I am forever grateful for that. In turn, I hope she spreads her wings and embraces the greatness within her spirit as she takes the next step on her journey.

As for me, I am walking a brighter path these days. I am really appreciating things from a different perspective now. It is truly mind-blowing how the things that seem to tear your world apart in one instance end up becoming the very building blocks required to hold everything together in another. Realizing that my lack of balance was stemming from too many tethers was the aha moment that I needed to let go of everything that had been holding me back for so long. It wasn't people, their actions, my job, or my boss. It was me. I had been allowing all the things I was holding onto from the past to corrupt everything I was trying to do in the present.

There is an old African proverb that says, "If there is no enemy within, the enemy outside can do us no harm". At some point, we have to ask ourselves what peace of mind is worth to us. You only have one life. Do not waste it holding onto things that will not make your garden grow. It's funny. The other day, I caught myself saying that today this stone has fallen into my garden, but oh how it adds character to the view. Even after we are gone, the garden we tend to during our time here will live on. Will your garden bear fruit for others to enjoy, or will it leave thorns to be tended to? Today, as I finish this text, I am patting the soil and leaving this seed for your garden. As you go forth from here today, tend to it well. The world can put so much weight on us at times that it feels like it breaks our plate altogether. So, I am honored to present to you, the plate that broke the world.

I hope this book blessed you in some way. There is a motto I live by that has served me well, so I will pass that torch to you as a way to say thank you for taking the time to read *The Plate That Broke The World*. "If you can be the spark that lights the way through the darkness for even one person a day in any shape form or way, it will not matter if your name isn't remembered throughout history. Your entire life will have been worthwhile." - Tucker Bearden

Tucker travels the country telling his story and along the way was recognized by Tom Ziglar, the son of the legendary Zig Ziglar. Tom took tucker under his wing and made him a Certified Ziglar Legacy Keynote Speaker & Trainer so that any time Tucker speaks, the Ziglars are there to stand behind him.

He was has been recognized as one of the top 30 speakers to hear in 2020 and beyond by Success Profiles Magazine.

Tucker Bearden

Tucker Bearden

Question: What does the word success mean to you?

Answer: Success is equivalent to "beauty is in the eyes of the beholder". I see success more as a path rather than a destination. Most people would say success is about money, fame, or talent, but I feel that someone's personal success should be defined as getting to do the thing that brings the most joy without taking joy away from anyone else in the process. Nothing brings me more joy than seeing people smile and hearing them say, "Thank you! This is exactly what I needed today".

I live my life by this motto: "If you can be the spark that lights the way through the darkness for even one person a day in any shape, form, or way, it doesn't matter if your name isn't remembered throughout history. Your entire life will be worth while" - Tucker Bearden

Question: What is your best habit or strategy you use to overcome adversity and obstacles?

Answer: When an obstacle stands in my way, I go beyond the point of ridiculousness! Smile! Get excited!

Make a fool of yourself if you have to, but DO THE THINGS THAT SCARE YOU! No matter what stands in your way, you have to remember that the only thing standing between you and the other side of pain is your belief that it is possible for you. Change happens in a moment, but that moment requires a process. When I was fighting to overcoming my life threatening anxiety, I would force my self into conversations with strangers over and over again. I made a fool of myself. I even had a few people who laughed and said, "Get away from us retard"...

Your WHY has to be greater than your current challenges. There has to be something you are fighting for beyond just making it to tomorrow. But no matter what it is, do not allow today to become tomorrow, and tomorrow to become someday. The obstacle you are facing might be a mountain, but even mountains can be moved if you will only begin to move the small stones you are strong enough to pick up today. They will make you stronger, and the stones that were once immovable will seem to move on their own. Take action! Have no shame! Control The Game!

Question: What advice would you give your younger self, knowing what you know now?

Answer: Smile in the darkness because without it, your light would hold absolutely no value. Pain is part of the process and it will not be easy, but believe in your heart that it will be worthwhile. The man you will become has very little to do with the man you were today, but it has everything to do with the man you are in this moment. So live for the moment and do the things that scare you! For when the moment is gone, you will never get it back.

Tucker Bearden is a Certified Ziglar Legacy, Keynote Speaker, Author, Aspergers Advocate, and Anxiety Expert. At eight years old, he was diagnosed with a neurological abnormality that hinders one's natural ability to understand social cues and emotional responses known as Aspergers.

Making friends and trying to understand people for him would be like someone dropping you in a foreign country with no translator and telling you to learn the language that day. Ironically, he found his passion after watching a TED talk and seeing the spark light up in people's eyes as they listened and leaned in close. A fire lit in his soul as he realized that this is what he wanted to do—to speak on stage and help improve lives with his story.

After nearly 8 months of battling his fear of speaking to people using pizza and a bicycle, he felt ready. After growing up deep in the sticks of Arkansas with a deadly fear of communication with others, he made my way onto stages around the country to show people that a diagnosis does not define who you are or what you are capable of achieving.

On this journey, he have endured homelessness, addiction, and bullying so intense, he has literally been doused with gasoline and chased through the woods with lit Roman candles.

This combined with several suicide attempts led him to where he is today, but most importantly, it made him realize that without the darkness, the light would hold no value. His challenges became his strengths and gave him a story capable of improving lives. There is no greater purpose in this world than service to others.

Erik Swansons Habitude Warrior Conference recognized him as one of their Top 7 Most Influential speakers and he was given a lifetime spot on their stages World Wide!

He created his own YouTube Channel to help people with anxiety called The Backwoods Buddha

Scan To Subscribe

THE PLATE THAT BROKE THE WORLD | 43

www.ingramcontent.com/pod-product-compliance
Lightning Source LLC
LaVergne TN
LVHW021742060526
838200LV00052B/3424